BOA
EDITIONS LTD

d-sorientation

d-sorientation

Charleen McClure

Foreword by Aracelis Girmay

NEW POETS OF AMERICA SERIES NO. 53

BOA EDITIONS, LTD. ∗ ROCHESTER, NY ∗ 2024

For information about permission to reuse any material from this book, please contact The Permissions Company at www.permissionscompany.com or e-mail permdude@gmail.com.

Publications by BOA Editions, Ltd.—a not-for-profit corporation under section 501 (c) (3) of the United States Internal Revenue Code—are made possible with funds from a variety of sources, including public funds from the Literature Program of the National Endowment for the Arts; the New York State Council on the Arts, a state agency; and the County of Monroe, NY. Private funding sources include the Max and Marian Farash Charitable Foundation; the Mary S. Mulligan Charitable Trust; the Rochester Area Community Foundation; the Ames-Amzalak Memorial Trust in memory of Henry Ames, Semon Amzalak, and Dan Amzalak; the LGBT Fund of Greater Rochester; and contributions from many individuals nationwide. See Colophon on page 97 for special individual acknowledgments.

Cover art and Design: Sandy Knight
Interior Design and Composition: Isabella Madeira
BOA Logo: Mirko

BOA Editions books are available electronically through BookShare, an online distributor offering Large-Print, Braille, Multimedia Audio Book, and Dyslexic formats, as well as through e-readers that feature text to speech capabilities.

Cataloging-in-Publication Data is available from the Library of Congress.

State of the Arts
NYSCA

BOA Editions, Ltd.
250 North Goodman Street, Suite 306
Rochester, NY 14607
www.boaeditions.org
A. Poulin, Jr., Founder (1938-1996)

NATIONAL
ENDOWMENT
for the ARTS
arts.gov

for Aisha

Contents

Foreword

d-sorientation—a feeling, a loss of bearings, a confusion about time or who or what or where. From the French "désorienter," literally translated as "to turn from the east," out of which we experience the rising sun. So that to begin Charleen McClure's book is to first stumble in the feeling, the word—sound and vision slurred, with the "i" both accounted for and missing. Stranger the word—the world now, shaped as it is by the urgencies of caretaking, tending to love across death, and the wisdom of multiple time-scapes existing all at once. In this case, shaped as it is by the devotion of keeping one's mother alive, and then the self—concepts more porous than my words here signal.

McClure's attention is most often with the inner rooms of selves and beloveds—entities present in pairs permeable to each other. A mother and daughter are also simultaneously a pair of mothers and a pair of daughters. Throughout, I read pairs of echoes, parallels, reflections and near reflections—fused as wishbones. As in: "My mothers' house has many mirrors." As in: "I huddled in that corner & that corner was my body…" As in one poem entitled "Caregiver" and another entitled "Caretaker." As in "d-sorientation" and "disorientation." Or how the essences of one entity ricochet like spirit through the poem, passing through the bodies of other entities, igniting in the speaker and the reader a new structure for thinking about what we are witnessing. We see this in the poem "barefoot in the snow." The mother recounts an often-recounted story of helping a woman, "static / wandering behind her / electric eyes," back home to her family down the road, "that didn't notice / she'd gone / missing." The mother sees her potential parallel in this woman in the snow and the daughter notes that where they live now it is not snow but "cotton / that frosts the fields." The daughter retells this story in the new weather of their lives together, translating the snow of the original story into the geographies and conditions of their lives together:

snow grows
from seeds in spring
and summer, from seeds inside
my mother. when I

retell this story,
i am the woman
in the snow of my mother's

cancer—

In this way, each of the story's subjects are, in the exquisite at-
tention of McClure, refracted by memory, illness, and time. This
refraction introduces new ways of understanding, even sensing,
the cancer, the mother, the woman. Reminding me of the poet-
ics of Lucille Clifton, such a poem creates a kind of inexhaust-
ible circuitry of relation between the subjects where an inferred
cosmology might begin to take hold in our reading. For example,
not only do I think of the relationship between cotton and snow
and cancer, but also the "seeds in spring / and summer" touch the
"seeds inside / [the] mother." Mother is kin with the seasons. The
seeds inside are kin not only with the cotton, but with the child
(also once-seed), now woman, now grown in the snows.

In even sparser works, the texts emerge out of a differently ef-
fortful and forged deviation. There are moments in "Mosquito,"
for example, when the pressure put upon the word sometimes
emphasizes gesture, or the sense that McClure is writing an
emergence. I *feel* echoes of M. NourbeSe Philip's "She Tries Her
Tongue; Her Silence Softly Breaks." "Ashes of once in what was /
...Silence":

can you taste—

her head shaking

—through me—

In "On the West I," an erasure of William Fox's 1792 pamphlet "An Address to the People of Great Britain on the Propriety of Abstaining from West India Sugar and Rum," McClure pursues the pamphlet into a different mode of language and un-language. McClure's work with the text is a collaboration, a lengthening, and an intervention. The pamphlet with which McClure is working begins with an eight-line rhyming poem entitled "The Negro's Complaint" by white English anti-slavery poet William Cowper and continues with Fox's 12-page argument for the boycotting of goods produced by enslaved African people. McClure's text enacts the ferrying of the pamphlet into a future moment of capital and empire, calling to mind Christina Sharpe's *In the Wake* in which she articulates "Black being in the wake as consciousness," proposing that "to be *in* the wake is to occupy and to be occupied by the continuous and changing present of slavery's as yet unresolved unfolding." McClure's work with Fox's 232-year-old text emphasizes the ongoingness of this unfolding and is something distinct and Black and beyond the pamphlet's frame, even as it is made, in part, of its conditions. In fact, it seems that in her erasure work McClure begins to hear a choral "we" whose language pressures the annihilating grammars of "the West," empire-making, and conditions of enslavement. McClure's practice and experience guide us to these imaginative, songful bursts of lyric steeped in touch, pain, intimacy, and political thought:

the West-I

with-held

under foot

She creates out of the page a material that is not actually "white space," but an inhabited field vulnerable to, and made out of, time. I sense experience here in the field that is recovered by erasure. Each page seems to draw from an accumulative charge made up of layer upon layer of time. For example, I sense that this wordlessness here marks thousands of gestures and traces of labor. Illegible and present. A sound beyond the sound that words can make:

                                        the least
portion of nourishment

no

rest

keeping pace

Throughout *d-sorientation*, McClure takes up the wondrous, painstaking and radical work of being in ongoingly deep relation with another through life and death, both vexed by and free of the thresholds. It is so moving then that the final poem of *d-sorientation*, "Transfiguration," is a series of unstopped, open lines. Sustained note(s) of a seriously steadfast and unending music, blessed are we to begin to know it:

leaving us the threads

of its forlorn music

We abandon all but this
one note which might mend

the harp aching at our ribs

:|:

aracelis girmay
oakland, california
2024

I.

orientation

this far: asphalt parting trees
but it's not the road you'll take.
travel ---th, then --st,
get closer.

geographically
map the liver, trapped
in his jacket as his stagger
suggests, an engorged address:
that he is your father,
your *daddydrowned* home.

visit the mother down the hall with both hands
beneath the broth. the coordinates beg you
to bring the spoon to her lips, metal on flesh,
the slope of her tongue, waiting—

Caretaker

She needs to eat. She needs
to keep something warm inside.
I reheat rice on the stove,
cabbage with smoked salmon,
and bring it to her in bed.
Like a widow, she chews the end
of a bone already buried. Ignores
the plate. I make her sit up anyways
adjust just before she spits
her last meal into my hands. Warm,
half-digested ghost.

Downstairs in the kitchen
I'll eat from this plate:
the white grains cold and dead
pinched in my fingers,
raised to a mouth open, ready.

And I'll try to—no, I will:
I'll keep it down.

an inheritance

& hands with nowhere else to go,

I laid against the silence
inside me as a room
beneath my navel
filled with blood

*

in the saints' uniform, my mothers kneeled
in the house of the lord. At his feet,
their prayers thickened

> their palm pressed
> as my body split
> into symmetry

they held me
in their arms
full of God

> as the cracked leather bible
> or weathered belt strap

*

in the heat of the swell, a well of red water—
but who was thirsty? who needed water like that?

*

mouth a holy *O*

*

I huddled in the corner & that corner was my body,
hair unraveled from pores

      thick threads curled
      into a skirt,
      a dark veil

*

they prayed and prayed and prayed

but how could I empty
my hands of myself?

*

My mothers' house has many mirrors
I can't escape
their bones—
      they live in my face.

Songs of Summer

the bills are due   the electric   the water   the gas and we're out
of milk the song plays from the car radio in soprano heat a full
choir of magnolia leaves backing the soloist two kids buckled
to the corners of her rearview   we return to the chorus   the car
pulled up at the red   light next to us toyota tuned to an old
year '97 '74 '88 '62 we've driven through miles of song   the tires
on a jc penny line of credit running low   the sunroof open and
just outside the window is my baby we're singing to   somewhere
spinning from here it didn't matter where we were going   past
the winn-dixie down old concord   cherokee shrub georgia
grown BOILED PEANUTS on a cardboard sign   salty lyrics
longing the pulp in our molars   the radio was on the windows a
blur of summer from the backseat   stalled on the side of I-285
at the roller rink it didn't matter the song crushed ice coca-cola
in styrofoam cups neon pink laces and a disco ball spinning
Freaknik in denim shorts white skates spinning   under our
feet concrete still spinning while spitting sucked sunflower
seeds in the parking lot   in the back of an old pickup as the sun
went down and the songs slowed on the waists of lovers as our
voices dimmed   rolling up the windows this late everything bent
into the black (black pines) (black deer) (the heart) car metal
dented against listeners calling in to stations this late between
songs is it more dangerous to love someone

Mosquito

blood moon
in orbit

close to skin

you know
the richest milk

is red—

*

proboscis insistent,
you subtract—lipids
                platelets
                protein

a balance that equals a hole
in the stomach

an ounce of the thirst I once was
                when my tongue searched
                for milk stirring beneath the skin—
                once latched on to my mother,
                I fattened til I grew a tooth
                and she stopped nursing me—

but look how I changed her
with my hunger

look how I charged her
with my mouth

*

the most important part
of the body is its pain.

can you taste—

her head shaking

—through me—

in what you swallow now?

*

at night in bed I lay
in the red lingerie
        of my veins—
beneath the fan's slow
blades I'm twisting in the sheets.

you visit with your slurred song
to unzip me from my sleep.

one bloodshot eye watching.

*

there is no relief—each bite
a city, a map.

I scratch the walls
searching for a way out,
but the buildings do not crumble.

I crush you in my palms instead,
and it's my blood on my hands.

*

you fill

       —as I empty
       each month
       from my center,
       blood that is skinless

       spilled milk

*

dengue
zika
west nile
malaria

*

what thirst makes a grave?

A Study of Human Effort

As much as we tried, it was not possible to bury her in the
human world. We laid her in the earth, blue planet that would go
on without us. We went to a future that would have us and slept

in the ruins we called home. As much as we tried, our memories
were never the same. For breakfast, she liked her bread barely
touched, lightly toasted. The edges left behind. Beyond the ache
of hunger, an appetite.

We went on.

With what weapons we had, we entered heaven. The bed was soft.
It kept our secrets intact, and our shadows by the fire. She said, *I
am my mother's daughter, oh, but I want to be alive*, and we heard
her say it. Six on one hand. Half a dozen on the other.

We were on both sides

of the gun. We decided there weren't enough daffodils to consider
the difference between living and hiding. We'd been given names.
We believed in time running out. The wind stirred the salt inside us

as we rested in the weather of stars. Their light fading, we sang
lullabies blue.

> *The cemetery is a field of flowers—look, how beautiful
> it grows.*

>> *Ripples 'cross the water, my little mortal heart skipped
>> like a stone.*

> *Forgive me*, we sang.

Forgive us since we couldn't forgive ourselves as much as we tried.

ON THE WEST I

Sighs

                                    the least

portion of nourishment

no

rest

keeping pace

.

the

        ground

        read
        one acre   as
                 re-

frain

the price

the price

the   price

of

sugar

is

murder   in

The large crop

language   explicit, and

"
"   possible.
"

"

"

"

"

"

"*more*." The day hardly dawns

                          or ceases

under

                    whatever   hands   pass thro'

                                                        the death

            we

rob

our

daggers

trembling

the West-I

with-held

under foot

                                                    the
                                            land refuse to

          quiet

in

the West

we suffer
to be held

;

the person called

to

is a question
with no   view

before us

The

    hood,   which   has   dis-
guised

      the

indigo

morning

be-
neath our notice,

is

the least de-
gree   of misery.

we extend our views to

the subject

bound

to   our minds

being "impossible

"

in that climate,

We

The

Dated

people

Salt

amp le in   other
States.

gimme the loot

       grease the geese   & gimme that good good
gold   spider in auntie's mouth   crouched high
    on the top shelf   near that bag of coins   yes
   i mean her tongue   cash   loaded—open
       the registry   open the cell   that door that
lazarus walked through
                        i want the money
making grandma's skin   fat pockets of air
    to share with the homies   that bread
where the ribcage splits like ships
     from the same port   sternum on lung & lung
        on beat   that vault   that bank of bone
   sewn in   the traffic of breath   & flesh that bodies
               obey—if i ask
         start the car   on everything i'd burn
        i expect   fools to keep they hands off
  my sisterbrothercousinand'em   i'm
  not asking   i'm slipping the rolex off the wrist
  of history   this ain't a game the flux and swerve
  law of paper states stacks on stacks on stacks
     past   present & future
  in a braid   like cane   or corn   cotton—
pay me: every song
      is about my baby's mamas
mamas mamas mamas mamas   since always

     & forever in my mouth   all of time
  all they eyes watching behind my teeth

II.

Queen Bee (gouache and cut paper on paper)

after Kara Walker

fertility will make us
        mothers—to be seeded and cropped.

we chose the dusk to run the field but clouds
of pollen glazed our skirts, made our bellies

titillate. at dawn they calculate abundance
        by the swelling. the most suffocating

body is queen: her tits, huge wooden spoon servings
of piquant. her stiff haloed nipples, a hive

a shack
        of heirlooms—honey

when she squats low, something like the sky
about her, watch them come out

                she births the shadows

Age

A

  wing
  ~~loving~~   or
  a   thing
         down   no
               ave

Here   he
             calling me

     ill   with
I don't mean to be old, but I   *know*
               for you and I can't

                    numb

his
                    number
                      ing
his   eve hang
                      it
Let me   ou t

        tonight

I gotta

Throw   down
his ~~loving~~

loving

                              reach

Come
  in
              to be

        nothing but

                                              change

Audible

> The wail is not my own
doing. It comes through me almost
by accident, like the horns on a passing
ambulance that echoes minutes later

a bruise in the ear. I hear it—
rising and falling in his chest,
my head against the memory
I stripped to be this close.

I was naked and in my nakedness, I
was stoic—a mute swan gliding into water
barely breaks the surface. He came
close. Because I wanted comfort

did he come closer.
The condom concealed
on the nightstand,
my ear against his chest,
the chambers of his heart
strained in silence latex thin.

I Bleed

through my night gown

into the sheets: the halo's crooked

crimson circles me. no—

                    I don't wear it

(like an angel) I ride it (like a horse).

blood is the saddle & I'm strapped

in: its animal, its mud, its hooves in

red clay the color of my waking.

have I crossed a line—maybe,

but it was in me all along

in the silhouette of sleep

where I was an open window,

where I was the rain's

collapse into petrichor,

unbecoming.

lovehunt

If the desert is naked

      it will worship

   no one.   If I am the desert, a tarantula

coils between my legs.

       I bring the married man   to my bed

          because he knows   to ignore the vows I make

   veiled in the dark   on my hands & knees his body before me

            posed like a church.

I go too far at night   roaming dry land

      until the stars appear   & he gazes at my teeth.

   I want him to spill   more on me

     than his jaw   tusks rising in the heat.

     When I sleep beside him, my eyes   full of sand,

I dream my love a wild boar   heavy & fat   breaths trudging

         a dense forest,

     I wound it with my arrow   crack its thick

coat of skin   I drag it home   I lug it to the table

like a bride before him   I let the light say *eat it*

    to its desert

leave its heart

        for no one.

Can anyone live with Eartha Kitt?

I cannot control who loves me or how
they do. I control
                        my jaw
its orchestra of bite and spit, if necessary
holding a man's bruised tongue
I'll chew.

-

The interviewer exhumes the contents: the funeral
and casket, the man waiting behind the door: suited, bouquet
of sealed lips. *The shovel* he tells her *is for you
to slip inside*
            you won't have your name, but you won't be alone

-

her face opens   her laughter   spits   she calls him a fool   her
eyes   narrowed to the scent of his sweat   she says I cannot
choose how I will die but I can choose what will kill me   she
lifts her shirt to breathe she lifts her shirt   to show him   to
give him a name for god: her chest arched forward for arrows

            a hole she whispers   *can give a key its purpose*

-

Ask the right question

            How do you keep warm?

I keep breathing. Listen:

        I keep breathing.

III.

Arrest

Hello, ma'am. We're the texas highway patrol. The reason for your stop is you didn't fail—you failed to signal your lane[1] change. Do you have your driver's license with you? What's wrong? How long have you been in texas?

Got here yesterday.

---

[1] tires rub away / white lines // crossing them / the road widens // green lights / nick the gas // the way / sirens imbibe // one's will / to pass // the car / stalls // the road / departs // you scan / the distance // for other routes

OK. Do you have a driver's license?

[inaudible]

OK, where you headed to now?

[inaudible]

Give me a few minutes.

[inaudible]

OK, ma'am. You OK?

I'm waiting[2] on you. This is your job. I'm waiting[3] on you.
When're you going to let me go?

---

[2] five SUVs / six trucks // one pedestrian / passing by // eleven /
sedans // three / heading south // nine / going north // likely / to
the highway

[3] a few cigarettes

I don't know. You seem very irritated.

I am. I really am. I feel like it's crap for what I'm getting a ticket for. I was getting out of your way. You were speeding up, tailing me, so I move over. And you stop me. So yeah. I am a little[4] irritated, but that doesn't stop you from giving me a ticket so [inaudible] ticket.

---

[4] a little / headway // the cigarette / yields // once ignited // it lends / a narrow // path / to the flame // you inhale // it / settles // into the softest / parts // of you / hidden from view

Are you done?

       You asked me what was wrong, and I told you.

OK.

           So now[5] I'm done, yeah.

---

[5] one road / becomes two // a lit / cigarette // divides / the path //
to smoke and ash //

You mind putting out your cigarette, please—if you don't mind.

I'm in my car—why do I have to put out my cigarette?[6]

---

[6] Who will answer / whose question // the cigarette / wavers // its smoke / off the tongue // the tobacco's slow / black track // turns / inward   flares // in the mind you / won't put out // fires 'cross the state / of texas // their ashes / question // their ashes / answer

Record

Can I get your name for the record?[7]

---

[7] What can these words do? I know you've been asked before. I've tried to re-wire the question into an invitation. I mean to invite you. And you see, I'm asking for a friend. I'm asking for a sister. Hey, sister, I'm not your officer. This question has no untimely end.

On Negation

Notwithstanding
minor annoyances—
      the enormous manor, noiseless
      footnotes on the linoleum
      anointing turnoffs,

      burnouts announcing
      nonsmoking tenors,

      monotony
      notwithstanding—

acknowledge
      notches, nooks, canoes

ignoring nostalgia
ignoring novelty
      November runoffs

ignoring nonessentials
      enough—

      another pinot.

      Not anxiety.
      Not nothing.
      Not now.

Noon—
nooses unknotted,
unanointed.
Knoll now pronounced
at the ankles now
        now
        now
knocking in a knot of girls.

The Bluest — Color Purple

after Kamilah Aisha Moon

At the slightest touch, leaves fall from branches—

Autumn. Dear God. Soon we'll disappear

behind the task we've been given.
Close the curtains. Clear the table.

Celie will trim Pa's hair while
Pecola washes dishes. Each submits

a humble petition to the chore: shedding
the fraying ends for a tapered crown,

casting the dirty plates to the basin
to shine as the pots shine,

a mirror for those inspecting eyes,
to fade as the surface fades to their image;

by their reflection, we depart
but by this devotion, could love be known?

And by this love, would we vanish
from the glassy stares of Mr ———— renting

the spare bedroom or the mayor's mansion,
from the eye-wide gap in the door

framing our mothers' glance off to work
or sick under the covers, vanish

from the endearing gaze of friends
who would forfeit their bikes to plant

a letter in our hands? Would it be better
than nothing? Would we vanish

as the last embers of Summer fall
to emerge in a patch of sun-

flowers drooping
on the outskirts of town

like long stemmed sisters
bending into one another

but falling, finally,
into themselves—

as dusk falls on bare branches
to cede the view to stars?

barefoot in the snow

my mother watches
a figure in the distance
in a coat and scarf

but no shoes on
the bare heels
she cuts through the snow.

she steps past
my mother's car.
the driver's door opens

to the static
wandering behind her
electric eyes.

my mother shuffles
with her,
elbow in palm,

back home
to family
that didn't notice

she'd gone
missing.
when my mother

tells this story,
she laughs at the end,
making me promise

not to let her go
walking barefoot
in the snow.

it becomes a joke
to slip in
with the season.

don't put me in a home
she tells me
with the money she loans

love me when i'm old
in the neat stacks
of clean clothes.

i shrug it off.
chances are slim.
snow is rare.

here, cotton
frosts the fields,
sleet flows

in windblown sheets
on clotheslines
beneath oak trees.

cocoons
ice their branches.
snow grows

from seeds in spring
and summer, from seeds inside
my mother. when i

retell this story,
i am the woman
in the snow of my mother's

cancer—

Caregiver

The midwife says *labor takes*
the time it takes, and years go by
in days—waiting. An egg inside her,
I was once a speck too small
for my mother to name or touch,
not yet alive enough to feel
apart from her feeling: bee stings?
love bites? loss maybe. The beating
of her heart my only measure,
the sound of her voice another room
in the house I'd yet to enter.

A child in the late afternoon
running to the door,
I crowned her with a necklace
of clovers strung together
while she was away all day
at work on her feet.
Gently, I rub them now.
She winces, her work not yet done.

I don't want to die.
I don't want to die, she says.
And she doesn't,
but she does the work of it—

and when the task is through,
I crawl to her side to kiss her,
my lips against the scar
on her left eyebrow.
I wrap my arms around her
to keep her warm, feeling
her fingers turn cold.

—sis draws a circle

A genesis.
An arc drawn
to embrace. Knowing
our youth would end
at the chain-linked fence,
we faced right.
each other.
My palm
a pulse against
yours. We
played a
game where
I reached
to catch
a hand,
to catch
a sister.

An ellipsis. Not all sisters
are born daughters, but all
sisters have been through it:
stretching the line to a curve,
weighing the line on a point,
catching the point in the descent
and the depression, curving
the line around to make ends meet.

We began
this way:
braided
to the scalp,
the lines
in our
palms
overlapping
as our hands met
applause.
We were slow to part. When the
nation, and the blood arrived,
clapping, our hands

A parenthesis.
The inner arch
of her left foot
mirrors the right.
She kneels
to draw.

Parataxis:
may she
return.

last minute approached in our
we were slow to part. No longer
were clasped.

The Sock Goes On

The sock is not mine, but I carried it home
a bundle in my arms. Just a few hours ago

I had let go, had closed the door on the sloppy
soapy water at the laundromat.

Limp, in front of the washer, in front of the dryer.
In the sack, a single sock. Not mine, a child's

not with years, but months.
The soft heat infant

of the dryer's *HIGH* cycle
orphan to a mother reaching

in the churning I pull from, I pull.
The single sock is not mine.

Rinsed,
spun dry: work blouse,

sleepwear,
moonlit. Not mine:

that sock, her white hat, the wool coat
that I buttoned on her at the front door.

Hug her heel around the boot.
Say: *Here, Baby. Open wide,*

the sock goes on before the shoe.

Ode to the Onion

soothsayer.
prophet.
you are the mystic's
clear eye

translucent
and faintly-veined
like spring.

you look kindly
on our kitchen tables
as you lead us into prayer.

we break bread. we pour oil.
we follow you through fire
to the edge of sweetness.

A Monastery for Alice Coltrane

She never say a word but I hear a storm:
the wind unsettling, american
cities in distress. It began with her wordless
moan eased on top piano.

Dear Alice, the cassava women
we come from taught us how
to pray, Sweet Alice
in california and open skies, Dear Alice,
I'm torn. Someone tell me how
'd the holy spirit get a hold—
                              I hear a storm.

Lord help me Lord help me Lord
help—I heard my mama yell some Sundays
Yes Lord, Yes Lord, My Soul
most others. I wondered if she ever fell
in love with a man who held his left
lung like a saxophone in detroit
or kansas city. Did anybody ever hold
my mama that way? Alice will tell about it.

She writes it down on her page
though the ink's not there
              as soon as she gets it all down, it disappears—
              as soon as she gets him down, he disappears again
              as soon as you get it down, it disappears
into the silence staining our hands. Scale the dream

of jazzmen, freshly polished shoes on sand,
the beloved posed beside them in the Sahara
next to pyramids; gold horns stretch
their hands.

I dream their lips pressed into song for the beloved,
into song for the creator, into song for us all.

At the monastery with Alice, we daydream,
doing the laundry, washing our clothes, throwing
the sun up and over our shoulder like trouble

Dear God

May there be peace and love and perfection
among all creation O God

May there be peace and love and perfection
among all creation O God

May there be peace and love and perfection
O God

I hear a storm

Transfiguration

Pull the strings from the piano
Is it quiet now—

Let's rest inside
the Steinway untouched

by the hammers of time

no beasts to be conquered
the ivory like a white-tailed deer

scurries off
leaving us the threads

of its forlorn music

We abandon all but this
one note which might mend

the harp aching at our ribs

Notes

"On the West I" is an erasure of a pamphlet, "An Address to the People of Great Britain on the Propriety of Abstaining from West India Sugar and Rum" written by the solicitor William Fox in 1792.

"gimme the loot" shares its title with a song by the Notorious B.I.G. It is the third track on his debut album *Ready to Die*.

"Queen Bee (gouache and cut paper on paper)" is an ekphrastic after a painting by Kara Walker entitled "Queen Bee."

"Age" is an erasure of "Age Ain't Nothin' But a Number" a 1994 R&B song performed by 14 year old Aaliyah and written by 26 year old R. Kelly, who in 2021 was convicted for sexual exploitation of a child.

"Arrest" is anchored in language taken from the transcript of the arrest of Sandra Bland by Brian Encina on July 10, 2015 in Prairie View, Texas. Bland was taken into custody and charged with assaulting an officer. Three days later, Bland was found dead in a jail cell. Officially, her death was ruled a suicide.

"On Negation" is inspired by "And" by Nicole Sealey, which in turn was inspired by the poem "Or" by Thomas Sayers Ellis.

"The Bluest — Color Purple" is inspired by Kamilah Aisha Moon's poem, "The Color Purple Rain." Its title merges *The Bluest Eye* by Toni Morrison with *The Color Purple* by Alice Walker. Pecola Breedlove and Celie are the respective protagonists from these works.

The midwife quoted in "Caregiver" is Elizabeth Davis.

"A Monastery for Alice Coltrane" borrows lines from "The Sun." It is the fourth track on *Cosmic Music*, her album with John Coltrane.

Acknowledgments

My gratitude to the editors and readers of the following publications in which versions of these poems appear:

Academy of American Poets: Poem-a-Day: "Caretaker";
Muzzle: "Queen Bee (gouache and cut paper on paper)" previously titled "Queen Bee," "lovehunt," "Can Anyone Live with Eartha Kitt?";
The Offing: "Age";
The Poetry Project: "gimme the loot";
Prairie Schooner: "Songs of Summer," "A Monastery for Alice Coltrane."

This collection is dedicated to Kamiliah Aisha Moon, a poet and dear friend. When you encouraged me to submit a manuscript to BOA's Blessing the Boats Selection in 2020, I told you that I wasn't ready. Next year, I said. The next year came and went. You passed with it. Thank you for planting this seed in my life. I have done my best to water it.

Writing is meditation. It provides space to be with what-is. But am I seeing clearly? Am I listening? Is my listening unobstructed? Are my perceptions? How do words, entangled with history and arranged by grammar's theatrics, interfere with my observations? How can I expose, interrupt, and collaborate with this interference? Can my senses withstand corruption?

The process is endless. The work is never done. But lately I think a poem is complete when it is shared—my thanks to you, dear reader.

My thanks also to aracelis girmay, for kindness; to Peter Conners, Justine Alfano, Kathryn Bratt-Pfotenhauer, Sandy Knight, and BOA Editions, for support; to Nicole Sealey and Mariahadessa Ekere Tallie for their brilliance and belief.

To Ama Codjoe, Ashley Lane, and Aurora Masum-Javed, for sacred care; to Ayesha Ali, Fatimah Asghar, Desiree Bailey, Sharon Baines, Jari Bradley, Mahogany L. Browne, Aaron Coleman, Sasha Debevec-McKenney, Gail Demchik, Lileith Dunkley, Tafisha Edwards, Bernard Ferguson, Rico Frederick, April Freely, Nabila Lovelace, Yona Harvey, Marwa Helal, S*an D. Henry-Smith, Luther Hughes, Raven Jackson, Omotara James, Ashley M. Jones, Quincy Scott Jones, taylor johnson, Empress Mahkeda Kellman, Sharon Kellman, Francis Logan, Esther Louise, Nabila Lovelace, Jonah Mixon-Webster, Yesenia Montilla, Saretta Morgan, Charan Morris, Nicholas Nichols, Hieu Minh Nguyen, Jordyn Penn, Xan Phillips, Gabriel Ramirez, Justin Phillip Reed, L. Renée, Wilton Schereka, Idrissa Simmonds-Nastili, Dominique Sindayiganza, Nawal Shadeed, Jayson P. Smith, Monica Sok, Paul Tran, L. Lamar Wilson, and Kamelya Omayma Youssef, for fellowship.

To the arts organizations that invested their resources in my writing, Callaloo Creative Writing Workshop, The Conversation Lit Festival, Cave Canem, New York University's MFA program in Creative Writing, Voices of Our Nation, the Watering Hole, and Women Writers in Bloom Poetry Salon; to those who offered feedback in workshops, the facilitators—Remica L. Bingham, Antoinette Brim, Robin Coste Lewis, Toi Derricotte, Natalie Diaz, Cornelius Eady, Ruth Ellen Kocher, Amber Flora Thomas, Vivee Francis, Rigoberto Gonzalez, Terrance Hayes, Janice N. Harrington, Lita Hooper, JP Howard, Erica Hunt, Tyehimba Jess, Nick Laird, Deborah Landau, Yusef Komunyakaa, D.S. Marriott, Dawn Lundy Martin, Eileen Miles, Tracie Morris, Gregory Pardlo, Willie Perdomo, Patricia Smith, Evie Shockley, Lyrae Van-Clief Stefanon, Kevin Young, Frank X. Walker, Rachel Zucker—and the workshop participants.

To Musa Jatta and the Jean Blackwell Hutson Research and Reference Division of the Schomburg Center for Research in Black Culture.

To The Rona Jaffe Foundation and New York University's Writers in Public Schools Fellowship for financial support.

To Sharon Olds, my thesis advisor, for compassion.

To Dr. Christine Cozzens, Dr. Waqas Khwaja, and the English department at Agnes Scott College for encouragement.

To my family for their patience; to my elders, Great Gran Nerissa, Great Aunt Mira—111 years old, my grandparents Busha, Carmen, Eulalee, and George, for the Word.

And to my mother, for eternity.

About the Author

A Fulbright scholar, Charleen McClure was a 2020 recipient of The Rona Jaffe Foundation Writer's Award. Her writing has been supported by Cave Canem, Callaloo Creative Writing Workshop, the Conversation Lit Festival, The Watering Hole, Women Writers in Bloom Poetry Salon, and VONA. She holds a MA in Teaching English to Speakers of Other Languages from Hunter College and a MFA in Creative Writing from New York University. She lives a few miles off the Chattahoochee River.

BOA Editions, Ltd. A. Poulin, Jr.
New Poets of America Series

Colophon

BOA Editions, Ltd., a not-for-profit publisher of
poetry and other literary works, fosters readership and
appreciation of contemporary literature. By identifying,
cultivating, and publishing both new and established poets
and selecting authors of unique literary talent, BOA brings
high-quality literature to the public.
Support for this effort comes from the sale of its publications,
grant funding, and private donations.

*

*The publication of this book is made possible, in part,
by the special support of the following individuals:*

Anonymous
Angela Bonazinga & Catherine Lewis
Mr. & Mrs. P. David Caccamise, *in memory of Dr. Gary H.
Conners*
Daniel R. Cawley
William Coppard
Jonathan Everitt
Bonnie Garner
Margaret B. Heminway
Grant Holcomb, *in memory of Robert & Willy Hursh*
Kathleen C. Holcombe
Nora A. Jones
Paul LaFerriere & Dorrie Parini, *in honor of Bill Waddell*
Barbara Lovenheim
Joe McElveney
Boo Poulin
John H. Schultz
Gretchen A. Voss, *in honor of Gary Conners*
William Waddell & Linda Rubel
Michael Waters & Mihaela Moscaliuc